Do you remember

THE BOOK THAT **TAKES YOU BACK**

BY

MICHAEL GITTER

AND

SYLVIE ANAPOL

CHRONICLE BOOKS
SAN FRANCISCO

DESIGN & ART DIRECTION:
Red Herring Design
Carol Bobolts
Kayt de Fever
Deb Schuler

PHOTOGRAPHY:
Archive Photos, The Bettmann Archive, Black Star/Stern,
The Milton H. Greene Archives, Photofest New York, H. Armstrong Roberts,
Schultz/Sunshine/Retna Ltd., Joe Steinmetz, Superstock Inc., Joe Wittkop

FLAP AND COVER COPY: Suzanne Falter-Barns

MANY THANKS TO:
Karen Alters, Peter Clemens, Patricia Eisemann, Rick Gell, Cindy Gitter, Erika Glazer,
Deena Greenberg, Caroline Herter, Paul Kowalewski, Emily Miller, Caryn Nathanson,
Robert Tucker, Paul Vaccari, our families, staff, friends and contributors around the
country, and most especially Dick & Dorothy Bobolts, Anna Mae and Leona Boboltz,
Darcy & Sean Fernald, Art & Mary Ann Knechtel, and Christine Grove for not
being afraid to search the dark recesses of their closets and garages.

Printed in Hong Kong

Library of Congress Cataloging-in-Publication Data
Gitter, Michael
Do You Remember? : the book that takes you back / by Michael
Gitter and Sylvie Anapol
p. cm.
ISBN 0-8118-1304-5
1. Popular culture–United States–History–20th century.
2. Popular culture–United States–History–20th century–Pictorial works.
3. United States–Social life and customs–1946–1970.
4. United States–Social life and customs–1971– I. Anapol, Sylvie. II. Title.
E169.02.G548 1996
306'.0973'09045–dc20   95—40709
CIP

Distributed in Canada by
Raincoast Books
8680 Cambie Street
Vancouver, B.C. V6P 6M9

2 3 4 5 6 7 8 9 10

Chronicle Books
275 Fifth Street
San Francisco, CA 94103

To E, Z, & A

Hub-i, Frub-iends!

(Or, for those of the post–Ub era — Hi, friends!)

This book began as a few simple reminiscences on a Saturday drive. The question at the time was Mystery Date—specifically, who was the preferred date, which somehow led us onto edible Creepy Crawlers and who sent away for the Muscular Dystrophy Carnival Kit. A good hour or so later a parlor game had been born, and it hasn't stopped yet. Since then, we've noticed a few things.

Once the question "Do you remember?" comes up, it is literally impossible to keep from reminiscing. It's almost as if you *have* to sit there and debate whether any of The Monkees could actually play the guitar.

Secondly, it appears there are certain experiences common to all American childhoods:
- the irresistible urge to unroll a Yodel
- small green turtles that lived in a plastic dish with a fake plastic palm tree on an island in the middle (note: the turtles always died)
- the smell of mimeograph paper
- losing Lite-Brite pegs in the shag carpet
- getting to stay up late on Friday nights to watch *Love, American Style*

Whether you put jimmies or sprinkles on your ice cream, the cultural experience of growing up in this country was essentially the same. This book is an historic work that celebrates some of the innocence, the sweetness, and the common connections of a time gone by.

Without further ado, it's sock it to me time.

Michael and
Sylvie

P.S. The pages here are organized randomly, like memories often are. If you want to see whether we've included your own particular favorites, though, check the index in the back. If it's not there, send it to the Do You Remember? Company for Volume Two.

5

MIA bracelets the women's
ERA Hanoi Hilton 1A status
draft dodgers burn the bra Huntley
streakers transcendental
Love Canal casualty reports on the evening news
Governor George Wallace

movement Gasohol Anita Bryant

leaded gasoline

& Brinkley the sound of the Teletype

meditation Walter Cronkite

"I am not a crook"

Aleksandr Solzhenitsyn The PLO

BEFORE CABLE TELEVISION

This Is Your Life Gomer Pyle Green Acres Lassie My Three Sons McHale's Navy Gilligan's Island Mr. Muir Candid Camera with Allen Funt The Ghost and Mrs.

REEL **1**

THE PARTRIDGE FAMILY

VIEW-MASTER
Stereo Reel

MADE IN U.S.A.

© 1971 and Trademark of Columbia Pictures Industries, Inc. – All Rights Reserved.

GAF CORPORATION
New York, N.Y., U.S.A.
T.M. Reg. U.S. Pat. Off.
Marca Registrada.

GAF Authorized User.

B 5691

1 Keith loved his 1952 Hudson, but it kept him broke.

2 He asked his mother, Shirley, for a loan, but she said no.

3 Keith left. Chris wondered why his mom was still talking!

4 Keith didn't have any better luck with Laurie.

5 "I'll lend money," said Danny, "if you let me be your manager."

6 At dinner, Danny announced that he was Keith's money manager.

7 It was time to leave for a singing engagement.

11

12

MYSTERY DATE Game

?

IS YOUR DATE BEHIND THIS DOOR?

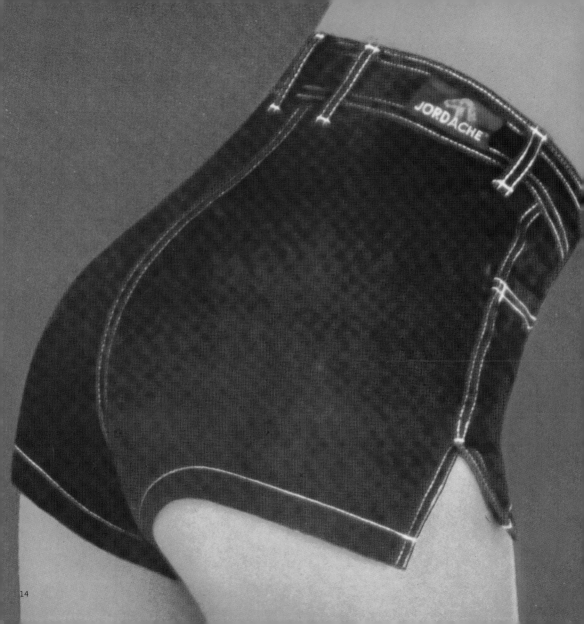

14

Sergio Valente Gloria Vanderbilt

"Nothing comes between me and my Calvins"

Sasson Knickers Levi's Bend Overs

bellbottoms bleach-blotched jeans

culottes tube tops bib overalls

Gunne Sax dresses Aigner basket purses

pantsuits gauchos minis, midis & maxis

ponchos halters Halston Izod Wranglers

 Ten-O-Six

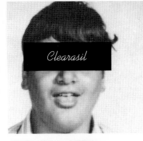 Clearasil

 green lipstick

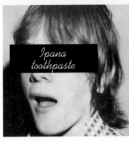 Ipana toothpaste

 Mr. Bubble

 CanoeCanoe

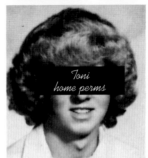 Toni home perms

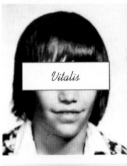 Vitalis

 Hai Karate cologne

 Stridex Pads

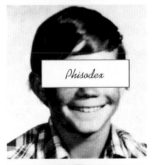 Phisodex

 Photo Unavailable

 Kissing Potion

 Avon Skin-So-Soft

 Halston 3-17

 Blue frosted eyeshadow

Afro picks

Shags

Beehives

Alberto VO5

Feathered hair

Teased hair

Short N' Sassy

Long & Silky

Wigs

Ducktails

Breck Shampoo

Clairol Herbal

Hamill Wedge

Sun-In

Ironing hair

Bangs

Dippity Do

Body On Tap

Pigtails

Nair & Neet

Farrah Fawcett hairdo

Pssssssst Instant Shampoo

Essence

Summer Blonde

"I told two friends and they told two friends and so on, and so on..."

"Gee, Your Hair Smells Terrific!"

Johnson & Johnson's No More Tears formula

"Which twin has the Toni?"

"Only your hairdresser knows for sure."

Lemon-up

Love's Baby Soft Shampoo

VCRs COSTING $1,000

CALLING AN OPERATOR TO DIAL LONG DISTANCE UHF

DITTOS BETAMAX

HANDHELD BATTERY–OPERATED FANS

CPM

BEFORE 911

WHEN ONLY DOCTORS HAD BEEPERS

BEING AFRAID OF MICROWAVES

TRANSISTOR RADIOS APPLE LISA COMPUTERS

LIFE BEFORE ATMS LIFE BEFORE ANSWERING MACHINES

PANASONIC LOOP RADIOS BEFORE FAXES

ONE PHONE COMPANY TURNTABLES

LIFE BEFORE CAR PHONES OSBORNE COMPUTERS TANDYCRAFTS

Manual Typewriters

ZAPMAIL BY FEDEX IBM PC,JR.

ELEPHANT DISKETTES CARBON PAPER

KAYPRO COMPUTERS

Jarts

Twenty Mule Team Borax

Swing Sets   "No more dishpan hands"

Beanbag Chairs   **Bunk Beds**

Rabbit Ear Antennas   **Tree Houses**

Frigidaires   Crock–Pots

Macramé Plant Hangers   **Waxing linoleum floors**

Pooper–scoopers   **"kalaka!"**

Bendix Washing Machines

Clothespins   **Wringers**

waxy yellow buildup   **Venus Flytraps**

Princess Phones

Newspaper Routes

Tupperware Home Parties

SPERRY AND
HUTCHINSON
DISCOUNT FOR CASH

Safari fold-up bicycles

Raleigh bicycles
streamers
Big Wheels
Columbia bicycles

3-speeds

handlebar bells

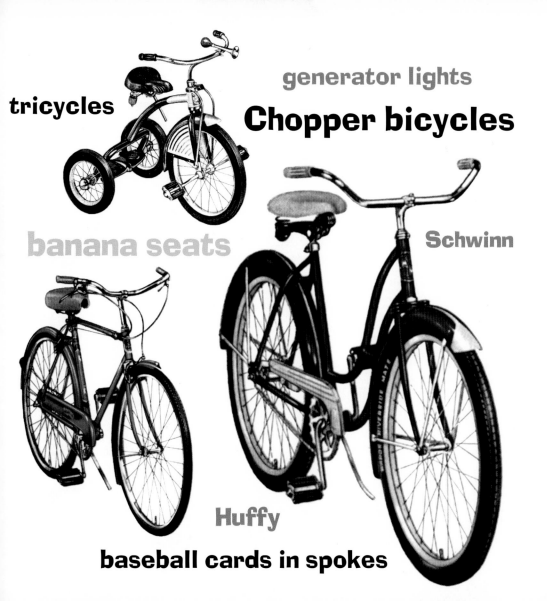

tricycles

generator lights

Chopper bicycles

banana seats

Schwinn

Huffy

baseball cards in spokes

chinese checkers

gyroscope

mexican jumping beans

slingshots

paper fortune tellers

kazoos

colorforms

hopscotch

shaker-makers

super elastic bubble plastic

rock polishing machines

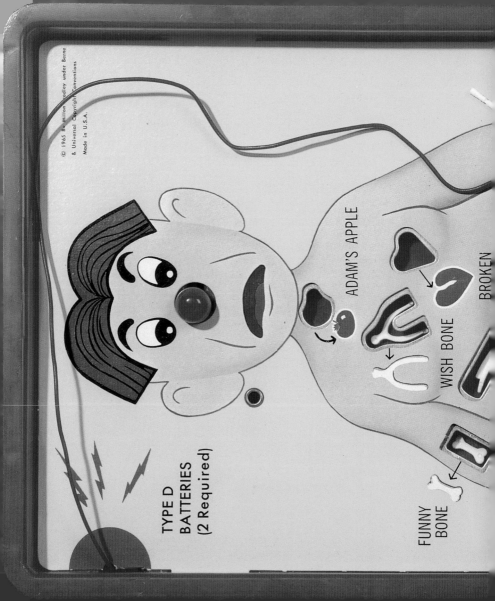

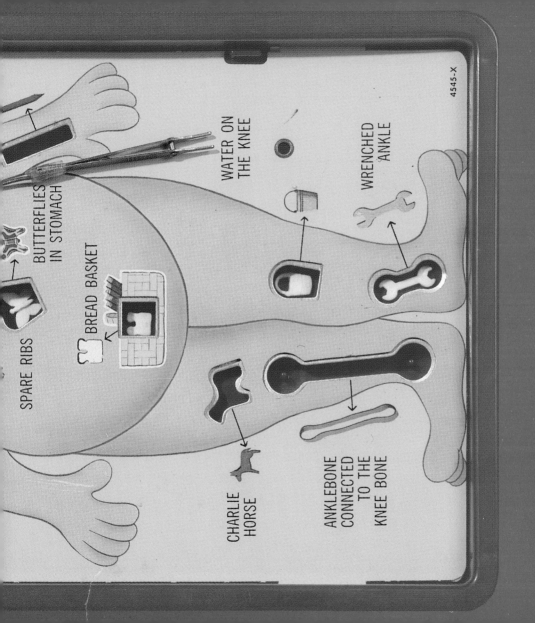

SPARE RIBS

BUTTERFLIES IN STOMACH

BREAD BASKET

WATER ON THE KNEE

WRENCHED ANKLE

CHARLIE HORSE

ANKLEBONE CONNECTED TO THE KNEE BONE

4545-X

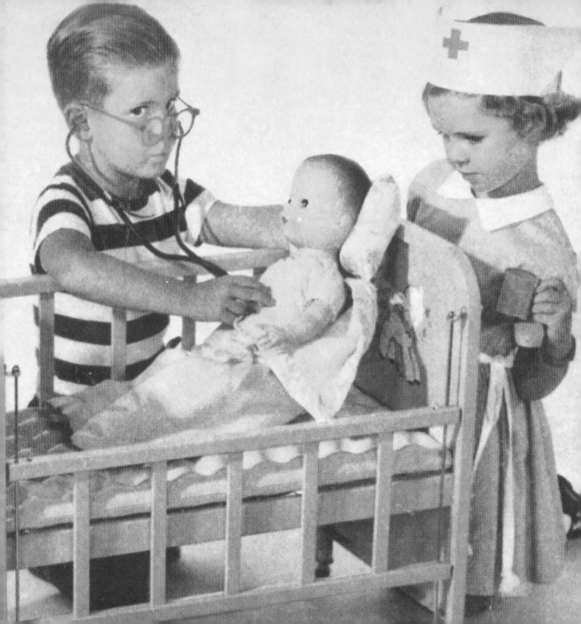

YOUR FIRST KISS

SPIN THE BOTTLE

SEVEN MINUTES IN HEAVEN

DEEP THROAT

balconies

Saturday matinees

cartoons before the feature

drive-ins

seeing your first R movie

before multiplexes

the machine that would drop the cup
after the beverage started to pour

ushers

smoking in theaters

PARAMOUNT PICTURES presents
A DINO DE LAURENTIIS PRODUCTION

JANE FONDA
SEE
BARBARELLA
DO HER THING!

Bye Bye Birdie **Planet of the Apes**

Jaws

That Darn Cat! **Flubber**

Godzilla

Fame Bob & Carol & Ted & Alice

Taxi Driver

The Parent Trap **Goldfinger**

Goodbye, Mr. Chips

The Graduate Mary Poppins

Star Wars

Easy Rider The Incredible Mr. Limpet

A Funny Thing Happened **The Exorcist**

on the Way to the Forum Herbie the Love Bug

Love Story **Valley of the Dolls**

Where Angels Go Trouble Follows

Catch-22 M*A*S*H* **The Godfather**

Quadrophenia To Sir With Love

The Computer Wore Tennis Shoes

Lady and the Tramp **101 Dalmatians**

Chitty Chitty Bang Bang

Willy Wonka & the Chocolate Factory

daisy chains
headbands
lava lamps
beaded curtains
god's eyes

MARY
HOPKIN

T R O
Organization
5 05
1801
X46416

HOSE
WERE
THE
DAYS

(Gene Raskin)

Produced by Paul McCartney

Time in a Bottle

Don't Be a Hero

One Billy

The Piña Colada Song

Kung Fu Fighting

Downtown

Classical Gas

The Night Chicago Died

Superstitious Let's Stay Together Theme from Shaft Proud Mary

Let Me Be There Pop Muzik Brand New Key Seasons in the Sun

Crocodile Rock Afternoon Delight Knock Three Times Fernando

Burn Rubber (Why You Wanna Hurt Me) ABC-123 We Are Family

Gloria Gaynor

light-up dance floors

Mirror Balls

Quiana

The Pointer Sisters

The Bump

Studio 54

STAYING ALIVE

Hooked On Classics

The Bee Gees

K.C. and the Sunshine Band

Saturday Night Fever

Xanadu

Donna Summer

Roller Disco

continues from step 12

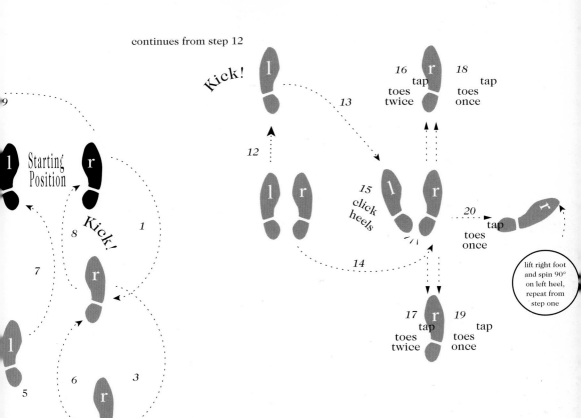

Kick!

9

Starting
Position

Kick!

8   1

7

5   6   3

13

12

Kick!

15
click
heels

16
tap
toes
twice

18
tap
toes
once

20
tap
toes
once

14

17
tap
toes
twice

19
tap
toes
once

lift right foot
and spin 90°
on left heel,
repeat from
step one

"Do the Hustle"

Bass Weejuns ○ Courreges boots

Chukka boots ○ Jack Purcells

Capezios ○ Earth Shoes ○ Vans

platforms ○ P F Flyers ○ Zips

saddle shoes ○ Mary Janes ○ Pumas

Converse Chuck Taylor high-tops ○ clogs

Adidas ○ Frye boots ○ Topsiders

Hush Puppies ○ Deckers ○ wedgies

patent leather ○ Bucks ○ Papagallos

Red Ball Jets ○ penny loafers

Double S sneakers ○

galoshes ○ flip-flops

Buster Brown and his

dog Tiger ○ Cherokees

"Right foot yellow."

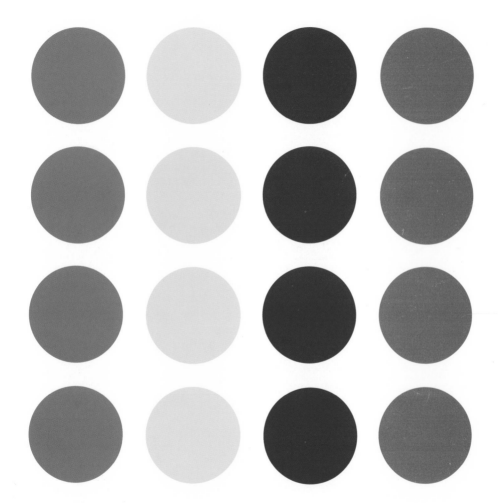

Losing Lite-Brite

in the ········►

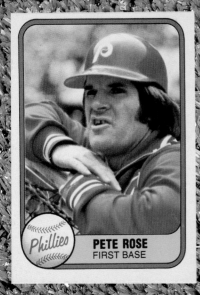

PETE ROSE
FIRST BASE

Jack LaLanne on TV

USFL Olga Korbut

Jim McMahon

Dr. J Pee Wee Reese

Mickey Mantle

Henry Aaron

Leon Spinks

Lew Alcindor

Babe Ruth

The Baltimore Colts

Earl the Pearl & Wilt the Stilt

Cassius Clay

Jackie Stewart Secretariat

Willie Mays

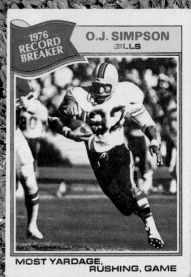

1976 RECORD BREAKER

O.J. SIMPSON
BILLS

MOST YARDAGE,
RUSHING, GAME

Ilie Nastase
Bjorn Borg
Tracy Austin
John McEnroe
Chris Evert
Billie Jean King
Bobby Riggs
Arthur Ashe
Evonne Goolagong

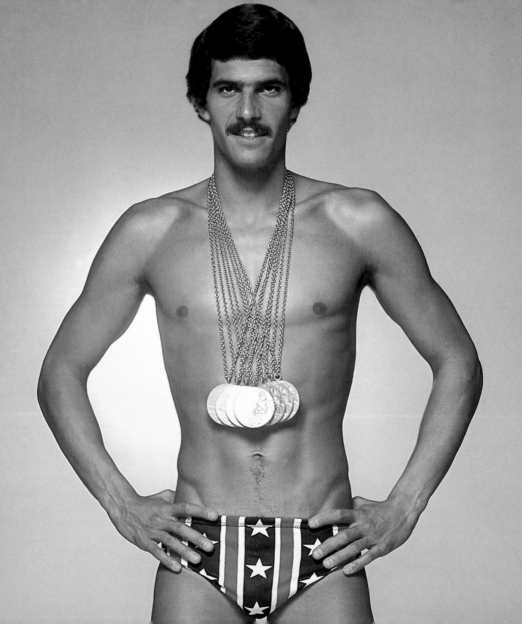

Israel's team taken hostage at the 1972 Summer Olympics in Munich • New York "Miracle Mets" • President Carter's boycott of the 1976 Summer Olympics in Russia • The "Thrilla in Manila" • American team wins Gold medal in ice hockey at 1980 Winter Olympics • Joe Namath dons pantyhose for L'eggs ad • Muhammad Ali is stripped of championship for not fighting in the Vietnam War due to religious beliefs • New York Jets win Super Bowl III (1969) to become the first AFL team to win the championship • Hank Aaron hits 715th home run to break Babe Ruth's record • George Steinbrenner fires Billy Martin—the first time • Roberto Clemente, hero of the 1970 World Series, dies in an Everglades plane crash on the way to help Nicaraguan earthquake victims • Miami Dolphins go undefeated in 1973's 14-game season and win the Super Bowl • Joe Theismann breaks his leg • Nadia Comaneci's Olympic "10"

Rubber Duckie, you're the one. You make bathtime lots of fun. Rubber Duckie, I'm awfully fond of you. **Rubber Duckie**, joy of joys, when I squeeze you, you make noise. Rubber Duckie, you're my very best friend, it's true. Every day when I make my way to the tubby, I find a little fella who's cute and yella and chubby. **Rubadub-dubby**. Rubber Duckie, you're so fine and I'm lucky that you're mine. Rubber Duckie, I'm awfully fond of you.

dinnerware from
the movies

terrariums

Popeil's Pocket
Fisherman

coughing ashtrays

Formica dinettes

Ginsu Knives

Seal-a-Meal

Dixie
riddle
cups

Gas Station
Glassware and Knives

Chia Pet

kaleidoscopes

head shops

patchouli oil

Incense

black velvet paintings

batik

Nehru jackets

Beatniks Cheech And Chong Fringe Vests SDS Gray Panthers Flower Power Woodstock

Haight

Central Park Be-Ins

Ashbury

LYDIA

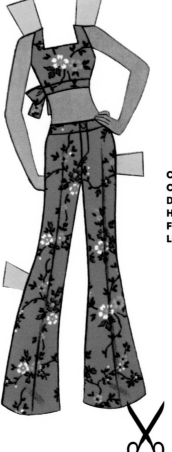

Kewpie dolls
Stretch Armstrong
Betsy Wetsy
G.I. Joe with Kung Fu grip
Mrs. Beasley
Malibu Barbie

Charlie's Angels dolls
Chrissie
Dressy Bessy & Dapper Dan
Holly Hobbie
Flatsy
Liddle Kiddles

ANT FARM

string art •

clay handprints • decoupage •

• woodburning sets • Heathkits

finger painting •

finger knitting

model kits •

stamp collecting •

• airplane glue

ght sets, with sensa-
ntrol for uncoupling
eel drive locomotive!

"Manumatic" Control—one of the new 1948 Lionel fea-
tures, found only in the colorful "Scout" line! Cars un-
couple going forward or in reverse at the pressure of
the "Manumatic" button. Track section to which control unit is affixed can be placed anywhere on layout.

LIONEL SCOUT

LIONEL

1007
LIONEL LINES

SCOUT

LIONEL

Baby Ruth

LIONEL LINES

Each "Scout" train includes
new No. 1011 Transformer,
with a power output of 25
Watts. Transformer uses A.C.
current only.

et. Cars have
"Manumatic"
or reverses by
ain set is 41½

er—1 No. 1002
ons No. 1013

$15⁹⁵

HT

y colored cars
, with realistic
r. Locomotive
. Extraordinary
421/2'66x 27⅜".
Tender—1 No.
007 Caboose–

1656

LIONEL LINE

No. 1656LT "027" AND "O" GAUGE SW
With Built-in AUTOMATIC BELL

This powerful, realistic Switcher Locomotive and Tender may b
separately. A perfectly-proportioned model of the "yard goats"

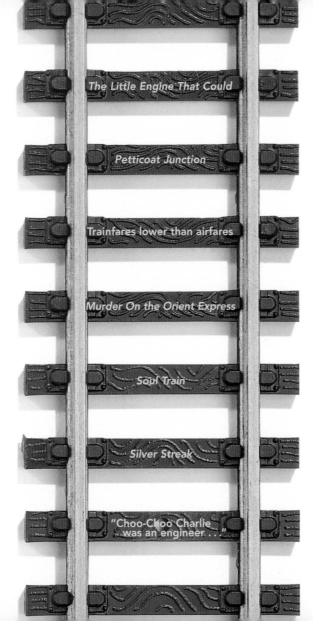

The Little Engine That Could

Petticoat Junction

Trainfares lower than airfares

Murder On the Orient Express

Soul Train

Silver Streak

"Choo-Choo Charlie
was an engineer . . ."

L   I

F E

B　　　　E　　　　F

O R E

F E D

E X

REGISTERED
STATE OF NEW YORK
MOTOR VEHICLE
REPAIR SHOP
TEXACO
OFFICIAL
STATE OF NEW YORK
MOTOR VEHICLE
INSPECTION STATION
BRAKE
Special
4 WHEELS
RELINED
99 9
Gas
State & Fed. Tax
Sales Tax
Total
INCLUDES ALL TAXES
TOTAL SALE
GALLONS
87
LEADED
GASOLINE
No OPEN No
GAS FOR GAS
SERVICE
AND
REPAIRS
ONLY

THE PACER

Yugos El Camino

DeLorean

Baby-on-Board signs Maverick

LEVI'S EDITION GREMLIN

"What's your handle?" leaded gasoline

DODGE DUSTER

Subaru Brat

"Are we there yet?"

Pinto

Datsun 280Z GASOHOL

AMC HORNET

dogs with bouncing heads

"10-4 Good Buddy"

VOLKSWAGEN THING

mopeds VW Beetle

THE RAMBLER Chevy Luv

simon · don't break the ice · ants-in-your-pants · cootie · kerplunk · hands
chutes and ladders · slime · wish-niks · vampire blood · silly putty ·

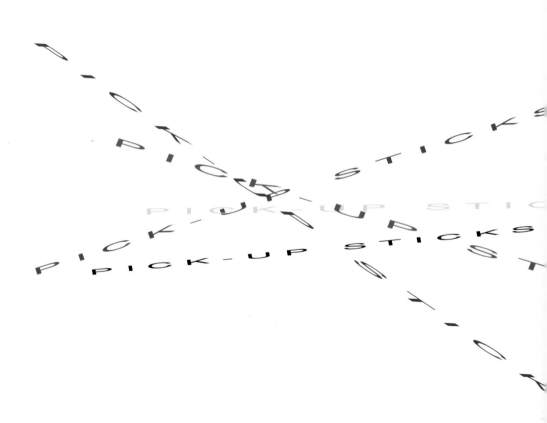

down • gnip gnop • hungry hungry hippo • wizzers
squirmels • trouble • mousetrap • magnetic football

the osmond brothers

the starland vocal band

tony orlando and dawn

the captain and tennille

peter lemongello

joey travolta

the hues corporation

olivia newton-john

tiny tim

kristy & jimmy mcnichol

elton john & kiki dee

the carpenters

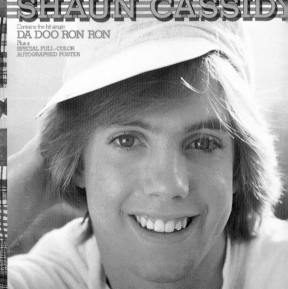

78

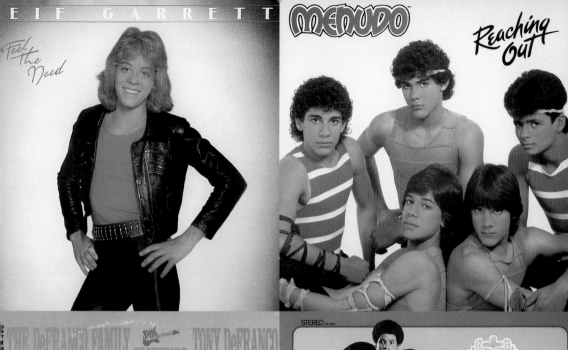

"I'm a little bit country…"

"… and I'm a little bit rock 'n' roll"

Charlie's Angels

The Man from Atlantis   Welcome Back, Kotter

Mork and Mindy   **Beat the Clock**

Let's Make a Deal Emergency!

The Gong Show

Baretta   **Don Kirshner's Rock Concert**

The White Shadow Lou Grant

Three's Company   Soap

The Tomorrow Show Adam-12

CHiPS Columbo

The Love Boat

Fantasy Island

Fernwood 2-Night

Truth or Consequences

"a three-hour tour" KOJAK

THE MIKE DOUGLAS SHOW The Dating Game

SIX MILLION DOLLAR MAN

ZOOM HOGAN'S HEROES

GRAMMAROCK

LAND OF THE LOST

THE BIONIC WOMAN

HAPPY DAYS

IT'S MY WORLD AND WELCOME TO IT

"PORK CHOPS AND APPLESAUCE"

 JAMES AT 16

"DANGER! DANGER! WILL ROBINSON" Match Game '74

Twoallbeefpattiesspecialsaucelettuce

eesepicklesonionsonasesameseedbun.

"I'd like to buy the world a Coke."

"It's Shake 'N Bake and I helped."

"Nobody doesn't like Sara Lee."

"I'd *walk a mile* for a Camel."

"I'd rather fight than switch."

"Ruffles have r-r-r-idges."

"Ho, Ho, Ho, Green Giant."

"Winston tastes good like a cigarette should."

"Plop Plop, Fizz Fizz, oh what a relief it is!"

"Ask any mermaid you happen to see . . ."

When it says Libby's, Libby's, Libby's on the label, label, label, you will like it, like it, like it on your table, table, table.

Oh Oh, Spaghettios!

How many? _6_   Take away 1.
                   How many left? ____

How many? _5_   Take away 1.
                   How many left? ____

How many? ____   Take away 1.
                   How many left? ____

How many? ____   Take away 1.
                   How many left? ____

How many? ____   Take away 1.
                   How many left? ____

book reports

lunch money

Your

bread and butter in waxed paper bags

kickball

First

the kid who ate paste

number two pencils

hall monitors

tetherball

Grade

little cartons of milk and graham crackers

spitballs

permission slips

Teacher

decorating lunch boxes

book covers

box of 64 Crayolas with sharpener

protractors

I pledge allegiance to the flag of the United States of America, and to the Republic for which it stands, one nation under God, indivisible, with liberty and justice for all.

Dick said, "Hello, Tom.

Hello, Susan.

Stop and play with Jane and me."

"Please do," said Jane.

"Come in and see our house.

I am the mother.

Dick is the father.

Sally is the baby."

Goodnight Moon Boys' Life

Highlights

Gulliver's Travels

Madeline Treasure

The Lord of the Rings The Five Chinese Brothers

Weekly

Dr. Doolittle

Curious George Charlotte's Web

The Cat in

Where the Wild Things Are

Pat the Bunny Peter

The Bobbsey Twins

A Wrinkle in Time

Misty

Ranger Rick

The Giving Tree

Island

Little House on the Prairie

Babar Eloise

Reader

Trixie Belden   Harriet the Spy

Judy Blume

the Hat   Winnie-the-Pooh

The Swiss Family Robinson

Pan   Black Beauty

HOLIDAY PAGEANTS

GOING TO BIRTHDAY PARTIES

LEAVING MILK AND COOKIES FOR SANTA

PLAYING DREIDEL

EXCHANGING VALENTINES

MAKING HAND TURKEYS

THE TOOTH FAIRY

THE LAST DAY OF SCHOOL BEFORE SUMMER

HANUKKAH GELT

TRICK-OR-TREATING

THE EASTER BUNNY

MUSCULAR DYSTROPHY CARNIVAL KITS

On my Honor, I will try:
To do my duty to God and my country,
To help other people at all times,
And to obey the Girl Scout Law.

Webelos
Synchronized Swimmers
Slumber Parties
Boy Scouts
Brownies
Red Plaque-detecting Tablets
Lemonade Stands
Playing Dress-up
Going to the Circus
Little League

The World's Fair
Standing on a Swing
Retainers & Head Gear
The Mumps
Piano Lessons
Crank Calls
Ballet Class
Recitals
Ig-pay atin-lay

HOW TO MAKE S'MORES

You'll need: 2 graham crackers,
1/3 of a 1 1/2-ounce bar of
milk chocolate, and 1 marshmallow

1. Toast marshmallow to a golden brown

2. Put it in a sandwich with the chocolate
between two crackers

3. Press together gently and eat

reveille

hospital corners

smoking behind the bunk

nametags in clothes

hats in the social hall

Sexton institutional food

treasure hunts

bunk beds

outstanding camper award

lights out

color war

archery

mess hall

canoes

collapsible water cups

care packages

canteen

t u g - o f - w a r

pre-addressed postcards

hiking

cookouts

being homesick

tents

telephone calls from home

softball

root beer barrels

flashlights
uniforms
mosquitoes
ghost stories
CIT's
arts & crafts
lanyard
shadow puppets
raids
sing-alongs
parents' day
water-skiing
pillow fights
muddy lake
cropsy maniac
medicine line at the infirmary
rest periods
sleeping bags
deepwater test
counselors bringing back pizza in the middle of the night
short sheeting
poison ivy
calamine lotion
bug juice
screen doors
taps

FIRE

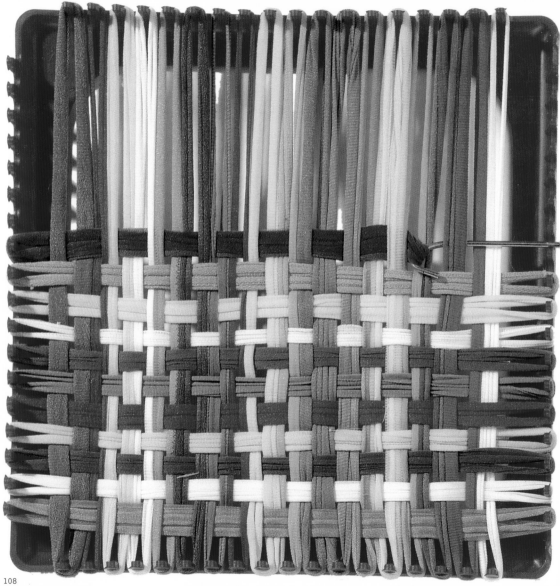

BATTLING TOPS

CHEERIO YO-YOS

CHINESE JUMP ROPES

EDMOND'S SCIENTIFIC

LINCOLN LOGS

MAD LIBS

SILLY STRING

TINKERTOYS

CREEPY CRAWLERS

Wonder Bread

Underwood Deviled Ham

Spam

Sloppy Joes

Shake 'N Bake

Hamburger Helper

Aerosol cheese

Rice-A-Roni

Vienna sausages

tuna casserole

pigs in a blanket

Eggo waffles

Cup-A-Soup

Instant mashed potatoes

Campbell's Soup

Tang

Hunt's Snack Pack
Rice Krispies treats
Reggie Bars
Dilly Bars
Devil Dogs
The Marathon Bar
Fudgsicles
Crazy Straws
Big Buddy Bubble Gum
candy necklaces
Jolly Ranchers
Jujubes
Now and Laters
Mr. Softee Ice Cream
all–day suckers
Ring Pops

Scooter Pies
Good Humor ice cream man
Fudge Town Cookies
Count Chocula and Franken Berry
Pudding Pops
Ring Dings
pink marshmallow Snoballs
Twinkies
Abba–Zabas
Zotz
jawbreakers
Good & Plenty
Fireballs
Pixy Stix
Candy Dots
SweeTarts

QUAKER®

QUiSP

Yogi Bear & Booboo

Kimba the White Lion

H. R. Pufnstuf

Speed Racer

New Zoo Review

Grape Ape

The Archies

In the News

Johnny Quest

Top Cat

Scooby-Doo

Magilla Gorilla

Secret Squirrel
& Morocco Mole

Fractured
Fairytales

Wonderama

SLAMO

Speed Buggy

Sherman & Mr. Peabody

Dudley-do-right

Space Ghost

Underdog

The Banana Splits

Shazam and Isis

Wacky Races

Tennessee Tuxedo

The Jetsons

Penelope Pitstop

Granny & Precious

Fat Albert & the Cosby Kids

Schoolhouse Rock

TOSS

Metal toys

Go Fish!

Hot Wheels

"You sunk my battleship."

flipping baseball cards

toy Texaco trucks

A C R O S S

wooden blocks

Creepy Crawlers

Hess trucks

Uno

Ouija boards

aggies and puries

here come de judge

Flying Fickle Finger of Fate Award

sock it to me

One Ringy Dingy, Two Ringy Dingies

very interesting, but stupid

117

"I can name that tune in four notes.

"I can name that tune in three notes."

"I can name that tune in two notes."

"Marjorie, Name That Tune."

Crying Indian litter commercial

Actually getting up to change the channel

"Makeup!" giant powder puff

Kitty Carlisle on "What's My Line?"

Black-and-white TV sets

Cigarette advertisements

"Carol, show us what's behind Door Number 3."

American-made televisions

"Beam me up, Scotty."

Late-night TV before infomercials

"Send it to Zoom, Box 350, Boston, MA 01234"

When TV channels went off the air at night

I'M SENDING CHESTERFIELDS to all my friends. That's the merriest Christmas any smoker can have — Chesterfield mildness plus no unpleasant after-taste

Ronald Reagan

see RONALD REAGAN starring in "HONG KONG" a Pine-Thomas Paramount Production Color by Technicolor

CHESTERFIELD *Buy the beautiful "Christmas-card" carton*

"HEY MIKEY, HE LIKES IT!"

"Ancient Chinese Secret, huh?"

"It's not nice to fool Mother Nature."

"WHERE'S THE BEEF?"

"I can't believe I ate the whole thing!"

"My dog is better than your dog."

"Is it a candy, or is it a gum?"

"They're Gr-r-reat!"

"It's a floor wax, it's a dessert topping."

"Puppy Uppers and Doggie Downers"

Babwa-Wawa

Samurai Delicatessen

Garrett Morris as Idi "VD" Amin

Emily Litella

Bad Theatre with Leonard Pinth-Garnell

"We are from France."

"Schwing!"

Live New Yo

"I'm Chevy Chase and you're not."

Mr. Mike Meets Uncle Remus

Saturda

"Vito, you're blocking."

Bill Murray as a lounge singer.

Jake and Elwood Blues

The Judy Miller Show

"We want your pollen."

"It's always something."

from

"Jane, you ignorant slut!"

"Ooooh Noooooooo. . ."

Chevy Chase falling down

ork, it's

Don Pardo

"No Coke, Pepsi."

"I am Gumby, dammit!"

Placenta Helper

Night!

The Widends

special prom noogies

"Land Shark"

The Not Ready For Prime Time Players

"We are two wild and crazy guys."

E. Buzz Miller's Animal Kingdom

North Central

Republic

Airport '75

before frequent flyer miles

Eastern

pianos on 747s

Braniff

People Express

Freddy Laker and the Skytrain

chiclets gum

the air-traffic controllers strike

before business class

crossing the tarmac and going up stairs to get on the plane

Idlewild Airport

smoking on domestic flights

New York Air

Capitol Air

The Trump Shuttle

painful headphones

metal "wings" pin

propeller planes

The Concorde

"

1. I have a dream that one day on the hills of Georgia the sons of former slaves and the sons of former slaveowners will be able to sit down together at the table of brotherhood.

2. That's one small step for [a] man, one giant leap for mankind.

3. In the future everyone will be world-famous for fifteen minutes.

4. We are not fighting for integration, nor are we fighting for separation. We are fighting for recognition as human beings. We are fighting for . . . human rights.

5. Power is the great aphrodisiac.

6. And so, my fellow Americans, ask not what your country can do for you; ask what you can do for your country.

7. You don't need a weatherman to know which way the wind blows.

8. When an individual is taken into custody or otherwise deprived of his freedom by the authorities and is subjected to questioning . . . he must be warned prior to any questioning that he has the right to remain silent, that anything he says can be used against him in a court of law, that he has the right to the presence of an attorney, and that if he cannot afford an attorney one will be appointed for him prior to any questioning if he so desires.

9. Nice guys finish last.

10. We know what a person thinks not when he tells us what he thinks, but by his actions.

"

1.H 2.J 3.G 4.B 5.F 6.E 7.C 8.D 9.I 10.A

A. Isaac Bashevis Singer
B. Malcolm X
C. Bob Dylan
D. Earl Warren
E. John Fitzgerald Kennedy
F. Henry Kissinger
G. Andy Warhol
H. Dr. Martin Luther King, Jr.
I. Leo Durocher
J. Neil Armstrong

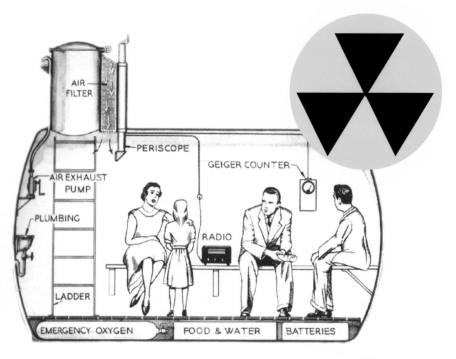

apartheid *Vietnam*

neutron bomb The Falklands

cuba before castro

Grenada SPUƚNIK

korean war Solidarity

drop/cover drill

NMARK

U · S · S · R

EAST
GERMANY

GERMANY

POLAND

CZECHOSLOVAKIA

AUSTRIA

HUNGARY

ROMANIA

YUGOSLAVIA

ITALY

ALB.

BULGARIA

T

TURKE

GREECE

crazy 8's

track tapes

millimeter home movies

Is Enough

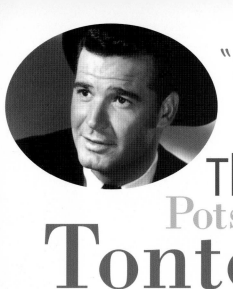

"Sit on it!"

To Tell the Truth Room 222

Gunsmoke Maude

The Flying Nun

Potsie F Troop

Tonto The Courtship of Eddie's Father

Julia Art Linkletter

The Mod Squad Uncle Miltie

That Girl Quincy

The Loretta Young Show Rat Patrol

Donna Reed Mission Impossible

The Fonz "Daniel Boone was a man, was a big man. . ."

Dark Shadows Bonanza

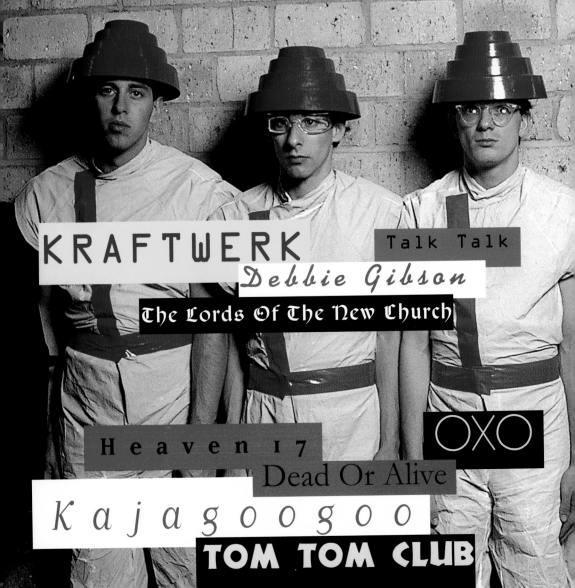

KRAFTWERK

Talk Talk

Debbie Gibson

The Lords Of The New Church

Heaven 17

OXO

Dead Or Alive

Kajagoogoo

TOM TOM CLUB

Yello

Alphaville
Haircut One Hundred
The Art of Noize
Ebn-Ozn
Men Without Hats
Thrashing Doves

ADAM AND THE ANTS

CULTURE CLUB
kissing to be clever

MEN AT WORK
BUSINESS AS USUAL

ABC
the Lexicon of Love

BLONDIE

a-ha

A Flock of Seagulls
The The
Split Enz
Bow Wow Wow
Kim Carnes
Quarterflash
Icicle Works
Dexy's Midnight Runners
Hipsway
The Outfield

HAVE A NICE DAY!

Didn't find *your* fondest memory
in **Do You Remember?**
Phone, or fax it, to us for
Volume Two at (212) 873-7223.
Or, e-mail us your suggestions.
Reach us on-line at
TakeUBack@aol.com
or on the Web at
http://www.doyouremember.com